A SHELTER FROM THE WIND

A SHELTER FROM THE WIND

VICTOR BOOKS®

A DIVISION OF SCRIPTURE PRESS PUBLICATIONS INC.
USA CANADA ENGLAND

Most Scripture quotations are taken from the *Holy Bible, New International Version,* ©
1973, 1978, 1984, International Bible Society. Used by permission of Zondervan Bible
Publishers. Other Scripture quotations are from (NEB) *The New English Bible,* © 1961,
1970, The Delegates of the Oxford University Press and the Syndics of the Cambridge
University Press.

Recommended Dewey Decimal Classification: 248.833
Suggested Subject Heading: PERSONAL CHRISTIANITY FOR WOMEN

Library of Congress Catalog Card Number: 91-65449
ISBN: 0-89693-883-2

1 2 3 4 5 6 7 8 9 10 Printing/Year 95 94 93 92 91

VICTOR BOOKS
A division of SP Publications, Inc.
          Wheaton, Illinois 60187

•CONTENTS•

• INTRODUCTION •

Being a prophet didn't exempt Isaiah from the winds of conflict. Being a Christian doesn't exempt us either. Isaiah had to learn to live for God, love God, and labor for God in the middle of some pretty dangerous storms. We can learn from his example how to make God a shelter from the wind and a refuge from the storm.

• BEFORE YOU BEGIN •

People who gather together for Bible study are likely to be at different places in their spiritual lives, and their study materials should be flexible enough to meet their different needs. This book is designed to be used as a Bible study guide for such groups in homes or churches. It can also be used by individuals who are studying on their own. The lessons are written in five distinct sections, so that they can be used in a variety of situations. Groups and individuals alike can choose to use the elements they find most useful in the order they find most beneficial.

These studies will help you learn some new truths from the Bible as well as how to dig out those truths. You will learn not only *what* the Bible says, but how to use Scripture to deepen your relationship with Jesus Christ by obeying it and applying it in daily living. Potential leaders will learn how to lead a discussion in a nonthreatening setting.

What You'll Need
For each study you will need a Bible and this Bible study guide. You might also want to have a notebook in which to record your thoughts

7

and discoveries from your personal study and group meetings. A notebook could also be used to record prayer requests from the group.

The Sections

Food for Thought. This is a devotional narrative that introduces the topic, person, or passage featured in the lesson. There are several ways it can be used. Each person could read it before coming to the group meeting, and someone could briefly summarize it at the beginning. It could be read silently by each person at the beginning of the session, or it could be read aloud, by one or several group members. (Suggested time: 10 minutes)

Talking It Over. This section contains discussion questions to help you review what you learned in Food for Thought. There are also questions to help you apply the narrative's truths to daily life. The person who leads the discussion of these questions need not be a trained or experienced teacher. All that is needed is someone to keep things moving and facilitate group interaction. (Suggested time: 30 minutes)

Praying It Through. This is a list of suggestions for prayer based on the lesson. You may want to use all the suggestions or eliminate some in order to leave more time for personal sharing and prayer requests. (Suggested time: 20 minutes)

Digging Deeper. The questions in this section are also related to the passage, topic, or character from the lesson. But they will not always be limited to the exact passage or character from Food for Thought. Passages and characters from both the Old and New Testaments will appear in this section, in order to show how God has worked through *all* of history in people's lives. These questions will require a little more thinking and some digging into Scripture, as well as some use of Bible study tools. Participants will be stretched as they become experienced in the "how-tos" of Bible study. (Suggested time: 45 minutes)

Tool Chest. The Tool Chest contains a description of a specific type of Bible study help and includes an explanation of how it is used. An example of the tool is given, and an example of it or excerpt from it is usually included in the Digging Deeper study.

The Bible study helps in the Tool Chest can be purchased by anyone who desires to build a basic library of Bible study reference books and other tools. They would also be good additions to a church library. Some are reasonably inexpensive, but others are quite expensive. A few may be available in your local library or in a seminary or college library. A group might decide to purchase one tool during each series and build a corporate tool chest for all the members of the group to use. You can never be too young a Christian to begin to master Bible study helps, nor can you be too old to learn new methods of rightly dividing the Word of truth.

Options for Group Use

Different groups, made up of people at diverse stages of spiritual growth, will want to use the elements in this book in different ways. Here are a few suggestions to get you started, but be creative and sensitive to your group's needs.

☐ Spend 5-15 minutes at the beginning of the group time introducing yourselves and having group members answer an icebreaker question. (Sample icebreaker questions are included under Tips for Leaders.)

☐ Extend the prayer time to include sharing of prayer requests, praise items, or things group members have learned recently in their times of personal Bible study.

☐ The leader could choose questions for discussion from the Digging Deeper section based on whether participants have prepared ahead of time or not.

☐ The entire group could break into smaller groups to allow different groups to use different sections. (The smaller groups could move to other rooms in the home or church where you are meeting.)

Tips for Leaders

Preparation

1. Pray for the Holy Spirit's guidance as you study, that you will be equipped to teach the lesson and make it appealing and applicable.

2. Read through the entire lesson and any Bible passages or verses that are mentioned. Answer all the questions.

3. Become familiar enough with the lesson that, if time in the group is running out, you know which questions could most easily be left out.

4. Gather all the items you will need for the study: name tags, extra pens, extra Bibles.

The Meeting

1. Start and end on time.

2. Have everyone wear a name tag until group members know one another's names.

3. Have each person introduce himself or herself, or ask regular

attenders to introduce guests.

4. For each meeting, pick an icebreaker question or another activity to help group members get to know one another better.

5. Use any good ideas to make everyone feel comfortable.

The Discussion

1. Ask the questions, but try to let the group answer. Don't be afraid of silence. Reword the question if it is unclear to the group or answer it yourself to clarify.

2. Encourage everyone to participate. If someone is shy, ask that person to answer a nonthreatening question or give an opinion. If someone tends to monopolize the discussion, thank that person for his or her contribution and ask if someone else has anything he or she would like to add. (Or ask that person to make the coffee!)

3. If someone gives an incorrect answer, don't bluntly or tactlessly tell him or her so. If it is partly right, reinforce that. Ask if anyone else has any thoughts on the subject. (Disagree agreeably!)

4. Avoid tangents. If someone is getting off the subject, ask that person how his or her point relates to the lesson.

5. Don't feel threatened if someone asks a question you can't answer. Tell the person you don't know but will find out before the next meeting—then be sure to find out! Or ask if someone would like to research and present the answer at the group's next meeting.

Icebreaker Questions

The purpose of these icebreaker questions is to help the people in your group get to know one another over the course of the study. The questions you use when your group members don't know one another very well should be very general and nonthreatening. As time goes on, your questions can become more focused and specific. Always give group members the option of passing if they think a question is too personal.

What do you like to do for fun?
What is your favorite season? dessert? book?
What would be your ideal vacation?
What exciting thing happened to you this week?
What was the most memorable thing you did with your family
    when you were a child?
What one word best describes the way you feel today?
Tell three things you are thankful for.
Imagine that your house is on fire. What three things would you

try to take with you on your way out?
If you were granted one wish, what would it be?
What experience of your past would you most enjoy reliving?
What quality do you most appreciate in a friend?
What is your pet peeve?
What is something you are learning to do or trying to get better at?
What is your greatest hope?
What is your greatest fear?
What one thing would you like to change about yourself?
What has been the greatest accomplishment of your life?
What has been the greatest disappointment of your life?

Need More Help?

Here is a list of books that contain helpful information on leading discussions and working in groups:

> *How to Lead Small Group Bible Studies* (NavPress, 1982).
> *Creative Bible Learning for Adults,* Monroe Marlowe and Bobbie Reed (Regal, 1977).
> *Getting Together,* Em Griffin (InterVarsity Press, 1982).
> *Good Things Come in Small Groups* (InterVarsity Press, 1985).

One Last Thought

This book is a tool you can use whether you have one or one hundred people who want to study the Bible and whether you have one or no teachers. Don't wait for a brilliant Bible study leader to appear—most such teachers acquired their skills by starting with a book like this and learning as they went along. Torrey said, "The best way to begin, is to begin." Happy beginnings!

1

Learning to Live

• FOOD FOR THOUGHT •

"There are so many systems of belief to choose from in the world today," a student complained, confused but sincere. "How am I supposed to know which one is right?" I appreciated his confusion and his sincerity. It seemed arrogant to tell him that Christianity was the "only" way to go. Yet the founder of Christianity Himself said, "I am the way [not 'a' way] and the truth [not 'a' truth] and the life [not 'a' life]" (John 14:6). I believe Him and so had no alternative but to present this young man with those facts. "Without faith in Christ's death on our behalf, no one "comes to the Father" however sincere he is. Sincerity alone won't get you to heaven, especially if you are sincerely wrong," I told him!

This particular student listened with obvious interest. He had no church background and had never had Christianity explained to him in a simple way. Later he committed himself to Christ.

It was a joy to reason together, to talk, to share, to wrestle through some things that were hard to believe, and to see this young person gladly put out his hand and take hold of life!

Later that same day I met with a woman who had been a believer most of her life. Married to a Christian, she had three lively children. She had drifted a long way away from her spiritual moorings and had allowed herself to become involved with a married man that she worked with. We argued and talked, and talked and argued, but nothing I said made any difference. Her mind was made up, her heart was hard, her soul was cold, and she had lost all respect for the church and the Lord! I couldn't reach her and watched her sadly as she left the restaurant where we had been talking and went her way. That day I read Isaiah 1 and realized that the sadness in my heart was nothing compared to the sadness in God's heart concerning His obdurate and stubborn child.

God reached out to Israel and offered them a dialogue—a chance to repent, return, and be renewed. Like the lady in question, however, they walked away from His gracious offer.

How is it that often people without the Lord are open and willing to listen and respond to Him, while people who perhaps have known Him for years refuse to listen and respond anymore? It's a mystery. The greater mystery perhaps is the love of God that persists in not only seeking the lost sinner but in also seeking the hard hearted saint! He offers life to both!

"Come, let us reason together," He says. This doesn't mean "let's have an argument"—as I had with my friend that day in the restaurant. It means to agree with His verdict about the heart condition of rebellion and repent of a cold, hard hostility against Him which is a result of deliberate sin. It means to acknowledge that one's actions have not been in accordance with divine reason.

After all, God's demands are reasonable! It is sin that is unreasonable. If we humans are God's creatures living in God's world, sustained and provided for by God, then to turn our backs on Him and go our own willful way doesn't make one bit of sense. Especially if we are true believers!

The Prophet Isaiah began his message to Israel by complaining that the Lord's people, who should have known better and been mature spiritually, had been behaving like a lot of sassy kids. "Why," the Lord says, "I get more respect from the animals I made than from you" (see Isa. 1:3). When God thinks He gets more respect from His donkey and ox—or in modern terms, His dog and His cat, than from us—then something is obviously very sadly wrong indeed!

There are few things more irritating than sassy kids. "My son shows no respect for his dad," a frazzled mother remarked, anxiously recounting a family row. "He sasses me all day long too!" A child who answers back rudely holds his parents with little regard and is not likely to obey them.

We modern Christians are in danger of doing the same thing Israel was doing. Some of us believe a half gospel, which means we accept the principles of Christianity without practicing them. We believe without the belief affecting our behavior in any discernible way. Jesus put it like this: "Why do you call Me, 'Lord, Lord,' and do not do what I say?" (Luke 6:46)

A short time after becoming a believer, I found out it was possible

14

to be a Christian chameleon if I chose, taking the color of whichever crowd I happened to be with! A young man came to talk with my husband one day. "I'm living with my girlfriend," he explained quite casually. "Do you love her?" inquired my husband. "Yes, I do," he replied. "Then why don't you marry her?" inquired Stuart. "Because she's not a Christian," he said simply! He didn't seem to see the inconsistency of his statement.

Complaining about Israel's inconsistent behavior, God says that even the daughters of the Philistines were shocked by their godless behavior. Somehow, even the heathen expected something more from those who professed to follow Jehovah.

Our world expects something more from us too. I was saddened to see a tabloid in the days of the Jim Bakker scandal that read, "The media opened Pandora's box and found Jim Bakker inside." A Christian young person wrote to her parents, "You'll just have to get used to my gay lifestyle and accept me. I still go to church and even attend a Bible study!"

Such examples of hypocrisy can lead someone else into believing false gospels or even no gospel at all! Israel had been chosen by God to relay His messages to the world. They were expected to be satisfied with God's revelation through the law and the prophets. They were forbidden to turn to magicians, soothsayers or diviners, yet even though the Lord God had protected, provided for, and led His people safely to the Promised Land, they had been all too ready to forsake Him and listen to anyone rather than to His chosen men.

No wonder Jehovah is distressed and says, "I reared children and brought them up, but they have rebelled against Me" (Isa. 1:2b). Their "whole head [was] injured," He said (1:5b). Twisted thinking led them to disrespect their Heavenly Father and disobey His word, and their sin had become like a spreading spiritual infection affecting their whole heart. Invasion loomed on the horizon and God's plan to use Israel as a means of blessing for the whole world was in jeopardy. No wonder God called upon His children to be reasonable, agree with His verdict concerning their backslidden state, and return to Him!

Calvin says that God's prophets were sent to proclaim the message of life and their words are surely as relevant and needed today as they were then. For those of us who believe in Christian principles without practicing them, who have allowed ourselves to believe a half gospel or buy into a false gospel such as the New Age movement—the Lord has thrown out a challenge. Such a departure from strict obedience and submission to Him alone is sin! This sin, the Lord says, is crimson which means "double dyed" (see Isa. 1:18).

15

When cloth was double dyed, it was an exceptionally deep crimson and, humanly speaking, was impossible to change. Any departure from the tenets of our faith, as far as God is concerned, can only be forgiven by a miracle-working God. Only God can bring life into spiritual deadness. We need to turn our backs on so-called New Age beliefs. "I believe Jesus Christ was a medium," a former Lutheran told me earnestly. I pointed out that the Bible said Jesus was a mediator between God and man—not a medium—and in fact the Old Testament forbade such "New Age" ideas thousands of years ago. These are crimson sins, but "though they are red as crimson, they shall be like wool," God promised (Isa. 1:18). Only God Almighty can wash double-dyed sinners as clean as that!

There is no life apart from that given and sustained by Him who said, "I am the life." "In Him was life," said John, "and that life was the light of men" (John 1:4). To be enlightened to this truth and then set alight by the reality of it is to enjoy His life to the full—and more importantly, to become a beacon for confused Christians who need a clear call back to their spiritual roots. If we will be obedient and return to the Lord, we shall enjoy the best things in life (see Isa. 1:19); but if we refuse and rebel, then God will treat us as He treated Israel, and we shall lose the privilege of being light-bearers for our world.

•TALKING IT OVER•

1. Read Isaiah 1 through.   *10 minutes*
   ☐ What words would you use to describe ...
     God's heart
     Israel's heart
   ☐ Read 1:18 over a few times. How is it that
     Christians can commit *crimson* crimes against
     God? Discuss.
   ☐ The word "repent" is usually addressed to unbe-
     lievers. Does it sound funny when aimed at be-
     lievers? Can you think of another word we could
     use?

2. Look up the following verses and discuss.   *10 minutes*
   Leviticus 19:26b; 20:27
   Deuteronomy 18:10-14
   ☐ How strongly does God feel about these sorts of
     things?
   ☐ What should be our response?

3. Prayertime   *10 minutes*
   ☐ Pray for people who are unaware that their sins
     have separated them from God.
   ☐ Pray for people who are meddling with forbidden
     spiritual practices.

•PRAYING IT THROUGH•

Suggested Times

1. Meditate on Isaiah 1:18. Pray about it.	*5 minutes*
2. Pray for— ☐ sassy Christians ☐ sick hearted missionaries ☐ hard-hearted leaders	*5 minutes*
3. Praise God for His willingness and ability to forgive and cleanse double-dyed sinners.	*5 minutes*
4. Pray for renewed believers to carry God's message of life and light into the whole world— Africa Asia Europe Middle East Latin America	*5 minutes*

18

•DIGGING DEEPER•

Introduction to Isaiah

1. According to the book itself, who wrote all or most of Isaiah? (cf. 1:1; 2:1; 13:1)

2. Names held special significance in the Old Testament. Isaiah's name means, "the Lord saves." What does his name suggest about his life, ministry, and writings?

3. During whose reigns did Isaiah live and minister? (1:1) See a Bible dictionary for background information on each of these men. What prophets were his contemporaries? His attention was primarily focused on which country?

4. Consult a Bible dictionary, handbook, or commentary to create a time line of Isaiah's life. Include important dates, events, Hebrew and Gentile leaders, and prophets of his day.

722/723 B.C.

_____|_____
                               |

5. Write a one-page history of the setting Isaiah addressed. Include what was happening to Assyria, Israel, Judah, Babylon, and Persia.

6. Read Isaiah 1, keeping in mind that it serves as an introduction to the whole book. What two major themes found there do you think will be elaborated on throughout the rest of Isaiah?

7. Compare Isaiah's opening and closing words (1:2; 66:24). What key word common to both statements will help our understanding of Isaiah's message and the situation he faced?

8. On a separate sheet of paper, categorize three of the several illustrations from Isaiah 1. Whom or what is being compared or contrasted to what? How are they alike or different? What is the single major point of each illustration? Include a reference with each.

9. To what is Jerusalem specifically compared? (1:8, 21) What hope is there for her? (1:26-27)

10. Review Isaiah 1. What is the crime, condition (1:5), punishment, and future of Isaiah's audience? What are the national consequences to individual and corporate sin?

11. What two inadequate attempts have the people evidently made to obtain forgiveness and acceptability before the Lord? (1:10-15) Why wouldn't these have achieved their desired result—warding off punishment?

12. Eight action steps toward repentance and obedience are outlined in 1:16-17. What are they? In which are you personally negligent?

Isaiah 1:18
13. What change does the Lord desire for and require of His people? How does this verse reflect the two major themes of the book?

14. Obedience by God's people will result in blessing. How is this blessing pictured? In light of what is happening historically, what is being promised?

Reflection
How has your knowledge of God grown from this study?

What is the Lord desiring for and requiring of you today?

The principle, obedience brings blessing but rebellion brings disaster, is loudly repeated in Isaiah 1. Have you learned this lesson for yourself? Recall an example from your own life when the Lord taught you this truth.

For Further Study
1. Memorize Isaiah 1:18.
2. Do a word study of *reason* (1:18).

•TOOL CHEST•
(A Suggested Optional Resource)

NEW AGE RESOURCES

A popular and current system of belief is the New Age Movement. To better grasp its false promises and lack of reality, an adequate understanding of its beginnings, dogma, and influence is needed. *Unmasking the New Age* (InterVarsity) by Douglas Groothuis introduces the roots and rise of the New Age Movement, its major tenets and compares it to biblical Christianity. Groothuis' sequel, *Confronting the New Age* (InterVarsity), teaches how to recognize New Age influence in everyday occurrences in business, education, music, and psychology. Suggestions for combating its eroding presence and how to witness to its converts are made. *Revealing the New Age Jesus* (InterVarsity), Groothuis' third work, is a comparison of the biblical Lord Jesus and the Jesus of the Gnostic and New Age religions. These works will clear away any clouds of confusion for a loved one who is swept up with the novelty of the New Age premises, and will expose their similarity to very old Eastern thought.

2

Learning to Love

•FOOD FOR THOUGHT•

I was helping our daughter-in-law corral her four-year-old, two-year-old, and eight-month-old twins — no easy task. At last, after a long hard day, all were bathed, put to bed, read to, and prayed with! A heavenly stillness enveloped us. "If these kids ever rebel, Debbie, after all you do for them," I commented to their mother, "I'll knock their blocks off!" We laughed together. It was inconceivable that after the total 100 percent commitment of each twenty-four hours of loving mothering, these children would ever be anything other than thankful and grateful! Yet we both knew each little one had a will as big as our own; and even if everything possible was to be done the right way, that in itself did not guarantee their response.

"I reared children and brought them up," complained Jehovah, "but they have rebelled against Me" (Isa. 1:2b). The nation of Israel had grown into a bunch of disrespectful adults intent on balking their heavenly parent's wishes.

Equally unthinkable, yet tragically possible, is a different sort of rejection — that of a once-loving wife toward a faithful, loving partner. Throughout the prophetic writings, the picture of a cheating wife (1:21) is an oft-recurring picture of Israel's treatment of Jehovah. The deep violation and hurt engendered by this sort of behavior can perhaps only be understood by those who have themselves experienced it. A friend of mine, abandoned by her husband, put it like this: "I couldn't breath — the emotional pain was so intense."

When we become "lovers of the world" instead of "lovers of God," that is how He feels. "See how the faithful city [Jerusalem] has become a harlot!" He cries out (1:21). So we should have no doubt about the deep emotional trauma we inflict on God when we play around with His affections and willfully indulge in a love affair with the world.

It comes as no surprise, therefore, that Isaiah writes a long song on God's behalf and delivers it to Israel.

It is a sad song—a melody of unrequited love. It tells of a lamenting affection that is not reciprocated. It's about loving and not being loved back—and worse—it's about the infidelity of the bride.

Isaiah, assuming the character of the bridegroom, really gets into the pain of it all. The bride is treacherous and ungrateful; there are no flowers, no children, no joy.

He uses a picture of a vineyard and a vine. Yahweh is the owner of this choice piece of real estate. He is the husbandman who with tender thought has bought the vineyard for Himself.

Believers belong twice to Jehovah! He created them and He redeemed them (Isa. 43:1).

This brings to mind a small boy who with great care made a little boat and set it to sail down a river. Suddenly he lost it down some rapids. Weeks later he couldn't believe his eyes when he saw his precious possession in a shop window. Running inside, he argued with the shopkeeper that he had made it, so it was his. The shopkeeper chose not to believe him, and nothing would do but for the boy to buy it back! As he walked out of the shop, he was heard to say to his little boat, "Now you are *twice mine*. I've made you and bought you back again!" Israel was twice Yahweh's; created and redeemed, they belonged to Him. So do we!

This helps us when difficult things happen in the vineyards of our lives. Then it is His business to be sovereign—our business to be loyal. It's hard to "mind our own business," yet it's a weight off our minds to remember it's not our business we're minding.

Not only is He the owner of our vineyard, He is the lover of our soul. In Isaiah 43:4, He tells us He has loved Israel and that His people are precious to Him. To think of God merely as one who made and bought us may cause us to consider Him to be a little impersonal. But to know He is the lover of our soul changes things. "But how do I know He loves me?" you may ask. "I don't feel it." One answer to that is that His love can be seen in His care.

Isaiah's love song tells of a husbandman who chose a favored situation on a horn of a hill—a very fertile place to plant His vineyard. This spoke of the prosperous condition of the people of God because of His thoughtfulness and care. We in the West have been planted on a favored hill too. As it was the duty of the Jew to consider the blessings that God had bestowed on him, so it is the duty of the Christian. God's watchfulness is seen in fencing in His vine—in hedging it about in order to protect it from its many enemies, and in building a tower in the middle of it. The tower was used to keep an eye out for Canaanites, bears, and even little foxes that could get among the vines and spoil the fruit.

In the base of the tower there was usually a room built for the family who owned and worked the vineyard to live in at harvesttime. I like to think of this as a picture of the Trinity coming to live in the tower of our souls. God comes within us to watch out for our enemies, yet we also need to realize that He has come into our vineyards for other reasons. He has come to dig us over—to gather out the stones and clear away the things that would hinder the growth and fruit of the vine in our lives. I remember asking the girl that led me to faith in Christ what He would ask me to give up. "Only your sin," she replied! Sin in a believer's life is like rocky soil in a vineyard that needs clearing out.

After His Spirit's work prepares the soil of our lives, Jehovah plants us with the choicest vine, just as He planted Israel.

In the Old Testament, the men of Judah were His pleasant plant. In the New Testament, Jesus is the true vine—as opposed to the false one (John 15:1). God expects us to produce fruit—and He certainly has every right to do so. As Isaiah asks Israel rhetorically, "What more could He do than He has already done?" He asks us the same question. He has just cause to expect holiness of character and lifestyle from us.

It should come as no surprise then to find a winepress in our vineyard. What sort of vineyard is it without one of these? When people are trampling all over our emotions, or we feel a crushing load like a giant stone squeezing the very life out of us, or the sour bunch of grapes of which we are a part is pressuring us—we are to count it all joy! This is the end that Jehovah looks for. The idea is to be pressured into producing sweet wine in order that our hopeless world may celebrate!

"Children don't create your attitude; they simply reveal it," a friend remarked to me after a particularly trying day many years ago. I wish she hadn't said that, but I knew it was true! As a young mom, I was aware that the pressures of motherhood would "squeeze" out of me either the sweet fruit of the wine—or the sour grapes of my own selfish nature.

Why did Isaiah sing his sad song to Israel? Because the nation had lost sight of the Owner's purpose for their lives and had become infatuated with another lover. And why do we need to hear Isaiah's song as well? Because we do not allow Jesus to reproduce His life through our branches. We too have lost sight of His purpose for our lives.

We spend our time whining, "Don't pressure me—don't prune me," instead of saying, "Oh, it's winepress time—a chance to give others cause for celebration."

> Pressure pounding
> Pain-again
> Sun and knife and wind and rain
> Husbandman
> attends His vine
> looks for fruit
> in His good time.
> Pruning, digging deep inside
> Stones revealed I've tried to hide.
> Dig me, make my life complete.
> Grow in me grapes
> luscious, sweet.
> Help me when
> I suffer loss,
> show me Christ
> upon His cross.
> Poured out wine was
> He for me.
> Make my life to honor thee.

•TALKING IT OVER•

*Suggested
Times*

1. Read Isaiah's love song (Isa. 5:1-7).   *10 minutes*
   What do you learn about God?
          Israel?
          Yourself?
   Discuss.

2. Read Isaiah 5:8-30.   *10 minutes*
   ☐ Discuss the sour grapes Israel was producing.
       Greed—5:8 and Leviticus 24:10-13
       Gluttony—Isaiah 5:11-12, 22
       Gurus—5:20-21
       Graft—5:23
       Grace—4:2-6
   ☐ Do you see these same dangers in the church
   today?

3. Reread the poem on the page before this. Pray   *10 minutes*
   about the lessons you have learned from this
   passage.

• PRAYING IT THROUGH •

Suggested Times

---

1. Praise God for His care of the vineyard of your life.
       the fence
       the hill
       the tower
       the pruning and digging
       the choice vine

5 minutes

---

2. Repent of the sour grapes in your life:
       greed, graft, gripes, and so on.

5 minutes

---

3. Pray for—
   ☐ Christians you know who are under pressure.
   ☐ Non-Christians who need to have the Trinity come and live in their *soul tower.*
   ☐ Yourself.

5 minutes

---

4. Meditate over John 15:1-8.

5 minutes

• DIGGING DEEPER •

Isaiah 5:1-7, The Song
  1. Read this passage and identify the following:

the singer

"the one I love" (5:1)

the vineyard

the jury

the indictment (5:4)

the punishment

  2. What specific words, phrases, and actions depict the Lord Almighty's feelings toward His vineyard? Where is the pivot in the story which anticipates change?

  3. List the six gardening techniques the Lord employed to secure a bountiful harvest. Were His expectations fair?

  4. What happens when you leave a garden untended and unprotected? Compare your answer to 5:5-6.

Isaiah 5:8-25, The Judgments
  5. Compile the woes in this passage. Who is being accused of what, and how are the recipients of these judgments characterized? The sentence for each offense is graphically outlined. Make a note of each.

6. Notice any bold contrasts in these verses. What is being highlighted?

7. Often there is some glimpse of hope among God's warnings and judgments. Can you find it in Isaiah 5?

8. Would the Lord direct any of these complaints to you? If so, concentrate on one to pray about and work on this week. Ask other group members to pray for you daily about this area needing improvement.

9. Write a synopsis of the *state of the nation* before the Assyrian take-over. Include a description of Israel's economic, social, spiritual, and moral condition (cf. Amos 2:6-7; 4:6; 5:11; Micah 2:1-2; Isa. 5:12-13, 20, 24).

Isaiah 5:26-30, Foreign Invasion
10. Who is the initiator and director of this attack? (5:26)

11. Even though these troops cover a great distance, what is the physical condition of their men, arms, and equipment for battle?

12. How is this army like a lion? (5:29) What response would this elicit?

13. How does chapter 5 continue Isaiah's two themes of salvation and judgment?

Reflection

Have you produced any bad grapes in your life lately? Or refused to produce what you know the Lord expects of you? Spend time in confession. Then list three action steps you will take to redress your wrong.

For Further Study

1. What was Israel guilty of in 5:8?
2. Consult a commentary or two for information on 5:17.

•TOOL CHEST•
(A Suggested Optional Resource)

APPROACHES TO OLD TESTAMENT INTERPRETATION
Do you seldom feel comfortable in the Old Testament? Perhaps you
enjoy the stories, but do not quite know how they connect to one
another. What is the New Testament's attitude toward the Old Testament? This tool helps the Bible student achieve an overall view of
the Old Testament and a greater appreciation for its purpose and
value in better understanding the New Testament. Not intended for
the novice, *Approaches to Old Testament Interpretation* (InterVarsity) by
John Goldingay will prove a challenge for the more advanced student
of the Scriptures.

3

Learning to Look Above

In the year King Uzziah died, Isaiah saw the Lord and wrote about it so we might be able to see Him too. Young King Uzziah had had a great start. Coming to the throne at the age of 16, he was discipled by the Prophet Zechariah. He was "greatly helped," as the Scriptures put it; "but after Uzziah became powerful, his pride led to his downfall" (2 Chron. 26:15-16). From then on it was all downhill for the king. He ended his life a leper.

Isaiah no doubt had sought the Lord on Uzziah's behalf many times during the 52 years of the king's reign. Knowing the man well, the prophet must have been bitterly disappointed when he failed to follow the Lord. Especially when he had had the benefit of such wonderful spiritual help.

It's in the year that our "King Uzziah" dies that we need to see the Lord too. Maybe we have a child like the young king who, despite the wonderful spiritual heritage we have given him, decides not to become a Christian; or maybe a loved one actually dies and we find ourselves mourning a family member or a familiar friend. Perhaps this is the year our marriage has died—or an engagement has been broken and buried. It is in a year such as this that we need to look above and have a fresh vision of the Lord.

Isaiah had a great desire to see God on His throne. He needed reminding that the Lord was in control of the situation. My husband used to sing a little chorus as a child that began "God is still on the throne." He got the words wrong and for years sang loudly and lustily, "God is still on the phone!" "Never mind," he said, relaying the incident, "God has a throne phone, don't you think?" He's certainly in control and He can undoubtedly contact the creatures He's created. We need to believe that in the year our world falls apart, and that *His* world is in perfect order even if ours isn't! The things Isaiah saw through the door of heaven will strengthen our belief as they strengthened his.

Isaiah struggled to relate the realities of heaven that he saw in human terms. Angels were singing a hallelujah chorus about God's holiness, and the glory of the Lord appeared. The very foundation of heaven was shaken at the incredible chorus of praise (Isa. 6:2-5). I ask myself: *If heaven is moved at the voice of the holy angels, what will happen to heaven at the voice of the holy God?* If we have a great desire to see God, we will; for He promises that those who seek Him with all their heart will find Him. We need to realize that if we *do* see Him revealed as we pray, or as we study His Word, or even in His incredible creation, we could be thoroughly devastated by the revelation. Isaiah's reaction to the sight of the holiness of God was to become searingly aware of his own unholy state. "Woe to me! I am ruined!" he cried. The idea of being ruined is similar to that of being unraveled—like a ball of wool that has come apart.

Having had a great need to see God and having had his wish granted, Isaiah now experienced a great need for holiness. The sense of unworthiness was overpowering. "I am a man of unclean lips," he lamented (6:5). Now this is amazing to me. I could well have understood him crying out, "Oh, my mind," or "Oh, my heart," or even "Oh, my wayward feet," but "Oh, my lips"? Surely Isaiah was the golden-mouthed prophet. *The Living Bible* renders the verse, "I am a foul-mouthed sinner, a member of a sinful, foul-mouthed race." Perhaps the effect of such a glimpse of God is to become aware, as Isaiah did, that even the very thing you do the best is unacceptable and totally inadequate in the presence of God!

To sense that our lips are soiled and to become unsure of the effectiveness of the things we do for God brings us as low as we can get. And if the things we do best will not do, then what about the things we do worst? Worship is a wonderful arena in which to discover how inappropriate our words have been or how inadequate our very best efforts are.

But God never leaves us kneeling before Him in a heap of helpless misery. He dispatches an angel from the throne to minister to us! He applied a cleansing coal from the altar in heaven to the very part of Isaiah's life that needed it, and said, "See, this has touched your lips; your guilt is taken away and your sin atoned for" (6:7). We don't know which ineffective sermon Isaiah was grieving over at the time or what words of witness or counsel he felt so guilty or inadequate about, but we do know that God cleansed him thoroughly.

Heaven's touch on Isaiah's lips was to result in some searing sermons in the days ahead. In fact you could say he became the original "hot lips"! Now he was ready for battle. Despite the political mess he knew was ahead in the wake of Uzziah's death, and in spite of his own personal grief, he had something new to tell the people of God. Having had a great desire to see God, and a great desire to be holy, he now had a great desire to be useful!

In truth, he was reminded that the needs of the world were Jehovah's great concern. As someone has said, "This is God's world and He wants it back!" The Lord asked, "Whom shall I send? And who will go for us?" "Here am I. Send me!" Isaiah responded.

How easy it is to say, "Here am I, so send my sister—or send somebody else." Even Moses said, "Here am I, send Aaron!" It's worship, however, that helps us to be able to make a right response.

Taking him up on the offer (God always does that, so be careful about what you say), the Lord immediately commissioned him to "go and tell this people" (v. 9). I can just hear Isaiah interrupting the Lord and saying, "Oh no—not *this* people!" How could God send him back to these particular ones? These people, God confirmed, were spiritually deaf, blind, and hard of heart (vv. 9-10). These were the very same obdurate people that had been resisting the prophet's message pretty effectively up until then. He must have wished he could carry the message to some other people that might be more responsive—to anyone else other than these! I think I can understand how Isaiah must have felt!

Shut up with three small children in my early mothering years, I asked the Lord to please involve me somehow in the cause of Christ. "Go and tell *this* people about Me," He replied. Confined as I was by my happy responsibilities, I knew that *this* people meant my near neighbors: the little old ladies who lived in the rose-covered cottages all around me. "Oh no—not *these* people," I muttered. I much prefer to work among teenagers instead of little old ladies who were blind, deaf, or who had heart trouble! Reading Isaiah 6:9-10, I clearly got the message to go and tell them anyway! It was only as I worshiped that I came to the point of obedience!

Starting off with three little old ladies—a deaf one, a blind one, and a sick one—God touched my lips and gave me a "hot" message for them. After much perseverance, the little old deaf lady came to Christ! In the ensuing months, dozens of others came to faith in the Lord through her. I learned after that to let the Lord identify the people that were my responsibility to reach.

It's hard to do God's work when you are struggling with hardhearted people who do not appear to respond to your message. When this is the case, it's going to take a vision of God, of ourselves, and of our world during our worship to motivate us to be faithful with *this* particular people. God, after all, does not call us to be successful, but rather to be faithful. So in the year that your "King Uzziah" dies, remember—God is still on the throne! He says to you, "Here am I—see Me." And the only adequate response to a sight of Him is "Here am I—send me!" May we all so respond.

•TALKING IT OVER•

Suggested Times

1. Read 2 Chronicles 26.
   □ What were some of Uzziah's accomplishments?
   □ What were some of his mistakes?
   □ What was the result of these mistakes?

10 minutes

2. Read Isaiah 6:1-10.
   □ What was one aspect of the vision Isaiah saw that must have encouraged him?
   □ Why do you think God chooses to use human instruments to do His work?
   □ If you were God, who would *you* use?

10 minutes

3. What aspect of Isaiah's vision do you think you need at this moment, and why?
   A vision of God
   —of yourself
   —of your world
   Who do you think God wants to send you to?

10 minutes

• PRAYING IT THROUGH •

Suggested Times

1. (Together) Meditate over Isaiah 6:1-4.
   Praise God for the things in these verses.

   5 minutes

2. (Alone) Meditate over verses 5-6.
   Pray for a spirit of repentance and for cleansing.

   5 minutes

3. (Alone) Meditate over verses 8-10.
   Pray a prayer of response.

   5 minutes

4. (Together) Pray for particular people in your life
   that need God's message.
   Pray for yourselves and each other as you witness to
   them—whatever their reaction or response.

   5 minutes

•DIGGING DEEPER•

Isaiah 6:1-13

1. If you were living at the times John F. Kennedy or Martin Luther King were assassinated, or during the Nixon impeachment trials, describe the political and social climate and the response of the public.

   Review your synopsis of Isaiah 5. What was happening economically, politically, socially, and spiritually when King Uzziah died? What might the Prophet Isaiah have been feeling at the time?

2. Look up the name Uzziah in a Bible dictionary. What facts are told about his life?

3. Read Isaiah 6:1-13. Describe the Lord's throne room and the activity therein. What similarities are there between Isaiah's vision and other throne-room visions in Scripture? (cf. 1 Kings 22:17-23; Job 1:6-12; 2:1-7; Rev. 4:5)

4. What were the functions of the angelic hosts?

5. No one has been permitted to see God and live, probably due to His absolute holiness and splendor. What was Isaiah's twofold reaction to his vision of God? (6:5, 8)

6. What three reasons did Isaiah give for his sense of foreboding? How did God remedy his problem?

7. What was foremost on God's mind here? On Isaiah's?

8. Put yourself in Isaiah's place. What spiritual truth does God have for you to learn from this vision?

9. What was to be Isaiah's message? What were the people to whom he was to preach it like?

10. How long was he to preach and how would he know when to stop? Who was the ultimate agent for the trouble to come?

11. What hope was Isaiah given to cling to in verse 13?

12. How does 6:1-13 fit with Isaiah 18?

Reflection
What is your response to be when you draw near to God? How has the Lord atoned for your sin? Hold firmly to His cleansing and ask the Lord to show you what service He has for you to do. Begin today.

For Further Study
1. What is the big idea or main thought of Isaiah 6:1-13?
2. What does this passage teach about Christian service?
3. Memorize Isaiah 6:8.

•TOOL CHEST•
(A Suggested Optional Resource)

DYNAMIC BIBLE STUDY METHODS

For those readers who love to really apply themselves to study, who long to dig deep into the Scriptures to uncover its treasures, who do not mind putting extra time and thought into their quiet times, Rick Warren's *Dynamic Bible Study Methods* (Victor) is tailor-made. Twelve varying approaches to digging much deeper into the Bible are outlined in detail in the pages of this very practical *how to* manual for developing fine Bible study skills. Warren teaches not only the importance of asking questions of the Bible and becoming a good detective, but also how to ask the right questions to divulge its rich and precious contents.

4

Learning His Lordship

Hezekiah was a good king. Having one of these was a change of pace for the kingdom of Israel! Good kings had been in short supply and Hezekiah had made a huge difference throughout the whole realm. When a good king came to power, he usually purged the leadership. The new leaders picked good people to serve under them, and the whole nation felt the impact. In other words, a wise king made wise appointments, and the appointees made wise decisions, and everyone in the kingdom enjoyed the benefits.

In this passage, Isaiah speaks about the reign of the future messianic king. We believe that Jesus is the Messiah; and when He rules the world, everyone will feel the impact! We know that this is certainly true in a personal way here and now. When the Lord Jesus Christ rules our individual lives and we quit fighting Him, then peace of heart and mind results.

Isaiah uses some graphic similes to describe what can happen. When the King is King, he says, "each man will be like a shelter from the wind" (Isa. 32:2a).

Christ needs to be the King of our lives for many, many reasons—not the least, for our own benefit. But we are blessed to be a blessing—saved to serve; and He intends us to allow His influence in our lives to reach far beyond our own personal needs. He wants us to be a windbreak—to stand between people and the stormy blast of all the devil would do to them to sweep them off their feet. In other words, He wants us to learn how to take some of the impact of the lashings of life for other people. He wants us to be a windbreak.

After all, Jesus was our windbreak. As our Savior, He bore the storm of God's judgment so we sinners could be saved from God's wrath. When we thank God for that and ask Him to forgive us for Christ's sake, He does. Then He sends us out to be like Christ, the sort of persons people run to when the storm comes. Can you think of people who are "safe" to go to, to confide in, to ask for advice? I'm privileged to know people who will stand with me in the problem times and will pray for me when I'm too confused to pray for myself. These wonderful people are people in whom the King reigns. They are a windbreak. I'm working hard at becoming one of those sort of people.

Each morning, before we go to work, Stuart and I reach for our prayer album. It's just a simple collection of photographs accumulated over the years from Christmas cards, missionary prayer letters, and the like. Faces of missionaries, family, friends, children, church leaders, staff, and neighbors smile at us. It's our "windbreak" album, and we stand in front of the devil in the name of Jesus and try to be intercessors on our friends' behalf so they will find a refuge from the storm. After all, Jesus did it for us—we can do it for others.

When the King is King, you'll find you'll not only have a desire to be a windbreak, but you'll want to be a watershed as well. Isaiah says that when the King reigns, "each man will be like . . . streams of water in the desert" (Isa. 32:2b). Now make no mistake about it: Jesus is the water—we are just the watershed diverting the river of life to the thirsty world around us.

This means we will see people with the Lord's eyes. People may look perfectly "together" on the outside, yet God alone sees inside and knows who is falling apart. There are dry, thirsty people all over the place—people who need a long, cool spiritual drink. As we learn to look at our world as He looks at it, we will become aware of a world panting for God. Granted, folk may not know how spiritually thirsty they really are; they may in fact be endeavoring to quench their thirst from dry wells, digging "broken cisterns that cannot hold water" (Jer. 2:13). So then it's up to us to be a watershed and divert the water of life in their direction.

Years ago when I was working with young people, I began to be asked to speak to women's groups. I really didn't want to. I loved my work with the kids and I wasn't sure if the ladies needed to hear the Gospel quite as much as the teenagers did. But God helped me to see the women through His eyes. I was reading Jeremiah one day and was struck by the prophet's great concern for the people of God. He knew the terrible things that were about to happen to Israel and particularly to the women. As he looked at their plight in his vision he said, "What I see brings grief to my soul because of all the women of my city" (Lam. 3:51). So I began to see women in this way too, and my soul and my heart began to be affected in the same way as Jeremiah's had been. Because the King reigns in my life, He gave me a heart for women; I began to be obedient to Him and take the opportunities given me to offer them a drink. Yes, when the King reigns, we will begin to be a windbreak and a watershed.

The last picture the prophet uses in this passage is that of a wall, a huge wall of rock. When the King is King, Isaiah says, "each man will be like . . . the shadow of a great rock in a thirsty land" (Isa. 32:2).

Of course, Jesus is the Rock—we are just the shadow of it. In the Scriptures, Christ is described as our Rock. In 1 Corinthians 10:4, the Bible describes the rock that followed the Children of Israel as they wandered in the wilderness as Christ. "He lifted me out of the slimy pit, out of the mud and mire," sang David; "He set my feet on a rock and gave me a firm place to stand" (Ps. 40:2). A rock speaks of security, stability, and serenity.

Sometimes it seems to me that the human race is running knee-deep through heavy sand under a searing sun. Some people seem to have been running for a long, long time and they are obviously at the end of their strength. Suddenly, a huge rock—the beginning of a mountain range—appears on the horizon. Rivers run down it, and trees grow around the base. What joy to reach even the shadow of the mighty rock within that weary land.

When Jesus reigns in the lives of true believers, they become like the shadows of that Rock. The dictionary defines a shadow as "an inescapable companion," and "an image of the reality." If we would mirror Christ, our Rock, then we too must practice the presence of God! The very best thing we can do for a weary world is to be like Christ. How does that happen? We get into the Word of God and find out what our Rock is like. We follow Him through the Gospels and learn His character. Then we imitate Him. We live as He lived—a compassionate, caring, helpful life. We give as He gave, speak out against injustice, help the poor, support the weak. If we try to imitate Him in our own strength, we shall fail, of course. But He has not left us to ourselves. He is indeed our inescapable companion! He lives within us by His Spirit to give us the power to live a Christlike life. This will bring hope to the hopeless, and help to the helpless, and joy to the discouraged.

I think of young children torn apart by their parents' divorce, or older children bearing young children out of wedlock, or old people forgotten by their families that have fragmented, too absorbed by their own traumas to care for them. I think of confused and empty teens, and individuals who are victims of drink, drugs, or all kinds of abuse. How much our world needs us to be like a windbreak, a watershed, and a wall!

Of course, if I learn to be a windbreak, I'll need to practice prayer till I become effective. And if I learn to be a watershed, I'll need to let the water of life flow over me first before I can be a refreshment to others. And if I am to be an inescapable companion of Christ, my Rock, I'll have to ask Him on a daily basis to cleanse my life of the sin that so easily besets me so I can have fellowship with Him and clearly hear His commands. It will all take time and effort. It will cost me — but then it cost Him! When the King reigns in my life, this is the very work He wants me to do. This is why He died for me and this is why He lives for me! The results of obedience will bring great glory to Him, great fruit in other peoples' lives, and order into the chaos of the kingdom that is ours. As Isaiah 32:3-5 says: "Then the eyes of those who see will no longer be closed, and the ears of those who hear will listen. The mind of the rash will know and understand, and the stammering tongue will be fluent and clear. No longer will the fool be called noble nor the scoundrel be highly respected." As we live lives of security, stability, and serenity, others will be drawn to us to ask why; then we will be able to tell them, "Because the King reigns in our hearts!"

•TALKING IT OVER•

Suggested Times

---

1. When the King is King

   Discuss the difference between accepting Jesus as your Savior and acknowledging His lordship in your life. Give personal examples.

   8 minutes

---

2. Being a Windbreak

   Discuss your prayer life. How much time is given to praying for others compared to praying for yourself?

   8 minutes

---

3. Being a Watershed
   - ☐ Read John 4.
   - ☐ Discuss Jesus' part in reaching a thirsty soul.
   - ☐ What can you learn from Him about being a watershed?

   7 minutes

---

4. Being a Wall
   - ☐ Do you need to show more of the *image* of Christ?
   - ☐ What one thing will you do to begin to make this happen?
   - ☐ Pray about it.

   7 minutes

•PRAYING IT THROUGH•

*Suggested
Times*

1. Make a prayer list for each day of the week.   *5 minutes*
   ☐ Monday—Family
   ☐ Tuesday—Church
   ☐ Wednesday—Work
   ☐ Thursday—World
   ☐ Friday—Anything
   When you have finished, pray through your list for
   today.

2. Pray about people you know who need the water of   *5 minutes*
   life.
   (first names only)

3. Pray for Christians to be more of an image of   *5 minutes*
   Christ.
   (no names)

4. Pray for yourself.   *5 minutes*

•DIGGING DEEPER•

Isaiah 32:1-8

1. Read Isaiah 32:1-8. Who is the subject of this passage?

2. What do we know about the leaders of Israel at the time Isaiah wrote? (Isa. 31)

3. Under righteous government, how would the general public be characterized? (Isa. 32:2-5)

4. What does this passage imply regarding how politicians are to serve their constituents?

5. A series of contrasts is found in verses 3-8. List them and determine the point of each.

6. Describe the character of a fool and that of a scoundrel (vv. 6-7). Add your own definition to each.

7. What is his government marked by? That is, if a fool or scoundrel were in charge of a country, what might it look like? (vv. 6-7) Who would likely be hurt, victimized, or made to suffer? How does this tie in to 32:1?

8. Governing officials were and are to be noble. Noble has been defined in one dictionary as "exalted moral or mental character of excellence." How is their nobility to affect their policies? (Isa. 32:8)

9. Reread this passage as if it were a satire. How does this add to your understanding of how to interpret these verses?

10. Should the public have a choice of what kind of men and women to put in office? Of whom is the public to be intolerant?

11. What kind of men had the people of Israel helped install?

Reflection
How can we avoid the same mistakes and poor judgments? What is our responsibility before God in the political arena?

For Further Study
1. Memorize Isaiah 32:2.
2. How does Isaiah 32:1-8 fit with 9:20?

•TOOL CHEST•
(A Suggested Optional Resource)

JESUS: LORD AND SAVIOR
Who is Jesus? What does it mean to call Him Lord? What has He to do with me? F.F. Bruce explores the heartrending questions asked by men and women for the last two millenniums. He shatters the glass menagerie many would like to leave Jesus encased in, adorning a shelf for show at home. This is a book you might like to read and then lend to a friend who is struggling to know the real Jesus—Lord and Savior of the universe, our "eternal contemporary," as Bruce so rightly calls Him.

5

Learning to Laugh Again

• FOOD FOR THOUGHT •

"I tried to run away from God," a teenager told me, "but I discovered He had longer legs than I had!" "So what happened?" I asked him. "I stood still and the sorrow in my life ran away instead," he answered. I turned to Isaiah 35:10 and we read it together: "Gladness and joy will overtake them, and sorrow and sighing will flee away." I explained that Jesus, who is our joy, delights to overtake us, stop us in our tracks, and give us something to sing, rather than sigh about!

God has given His people a spiritual inheritance, part of which is a deep experience of abiding joy. Joy strengthens us to serve Him even in the middle of trouble. "The joy of the Lord is your strength," the Bible says (Neh. 8:10). Isaiah speaks for Jehovah when he says He will give us "the oil of gladness instead of mourning, and a garment of praise instead of a spirit of despair" (Isa. 61:3).

The Children of Israel knew exactly what a spirit of heaviness felt like. Far away from God, they were living with the consequences of their own mistakes. Babylonian soldiers had taken them prisoner, transporting them to a strange country and forcing them to slave away for them. They had endured cruelty that is very hard for us to imagine, even when we live in such a violent culture ourselves. Children had had their brains beaten out against the stones, while adults were murdered or tortured. The Israelites, wearied with pain and sorrow and bitter with the blows they had been forced to take, were more than open to hear their prophet bring a word of helping strength and comfort.

Isaiah set about reminding his people of the facts of their faith. "Don't you know—haven't you heard?" he asks them. "Heard what?" they responded wearily. "God doesn't wear out," Isaiah replied. "Jehovah is the God of eternity that created the ends of the earth" (Isa. 40:28). Such a God lasts! This powerful One is never powerless. This changeless One never changes. He never faints or is fatigued.

Why was this such a great piece of news for these people? Because they were worn out, powerless and fatigued, tired out with the trouble they found themselves in. They needed to remember, as we do when we face trials, that when we have "had it," He hasn't. When we quit, He doesn't. When we let go of Him, He hangs onto us!

We get a good feel for the situation from Psalm 137:1-4. Sitting by the waters of Babylon, the Israelites had hung up their harps on a weeping willow tree! (see Ps. 137:2, KJV) In other words, they had lost their joy. When they thought of Jerusalem, a great wave of nostalgia flooded over them; and when they talked about their captors' cruelty, bitterness and a spirit of revenge engulfed them (Ps. 137:8).

To make matters worse, the Babylonians taunted them relentlessly saying, "Sing us one of the songs of Zion!" (Ps. 137:3) "How can we sing the songs of the Lord while in a foreign land?" the people responded (v. 4). Yet it is a song of Zion sung with joy in a foreign land that can be the most powerful testimony of all to lost people like the Babylonians.

The Christian who is gossiped about in the office but doesn't retaliate; the believer snubbed by her workmates who bears it with joy; the teenager left out of the group because of his faith who ignores the snub; or even the little child who is beaten up in the schoolyard because he refuses to fight—they are all singing their own song of Zion in their particular foreign land. "This world is not my home, I'm just a passing thru," the song reminds us. This world is a hostile place if you live your life in line with Christian beliefs. It's a place without too much to sing about. The person who knows the Music Maker will have a song to sing. It may indeed be a song in minor key, but it will still be a song.

Are we sitting by our personal waters of trouble, having hung up our joy on some tree of trouble? Perhaps we lost our joy at the gripe tree. We grumble away about anything and everything. Life isn't fair, we say. We complain about the church, the pastor, and the world in general. When we complain, our spirit is overwhelmed. If we are too busy complaining ever to be truly thankful, we are too busy!

A Chinese pastor spent years in a prison camp for his faith. He was assigned to the sewage pit. He testified to the "joy" of his assignment. For obvious reasons, no one ever came near him and this gave him the chance to sing praises to God all day long!

Perhaps we have hung up our harp on the guilt tree. Guilt doesn't know any songs. Harboring a grudge against someone who has wronged us wrecks any hope of joy. The devil, who is a murderer from the beginning (and, therefore, is a very real killjoy), makes sure we are wallowing in guilt whenever possible. If we are guilty, then we should confess our sin. God will forgive us, cleanse us, and restore our joy.

Perhaps we have hung up our harp on the grief tree. It must have been terrible for the Israelites to see their children murdered before their very eyes. Maybe drink or drugs have destroyed your children before your very eyes, and you are devastated by grief. Who can sing a song when they see their children suffering? An older lady said to me, "My daughter had an abortion. I was going to be a grandmother. Now I feel I've had one too!" There is so much grief in the world. Only a God of grief such as our God, who saw His own Child murdered, can write a song for us to sing in grief's darkest night.

Perhaps we have hung up our harp on the growth tree. Maybe we began the Christian life with zeal and fortitude but fizzled out somewhere along the way. Or maybe we lost our happiness at a much less traumatic place—the grind tree. Nazareth living is mundane. If we allow them to, dull, daily doings can take the edge off our enjoyment of life as God intended life to be. And there's the key: Joy is a command. "Rejoice in the Lord always. I will say it again: Rejoice!" Paul wrote from prison (Phil. 4:4). He meant "all" days, not "some" days.

Isaiah calls the people of God to confirm their weak-kneed faith (Isa. 35:3). He calls them back to patient waiting on the Lord, who is the source of their strength and joy—to exchange their weariness for His power, to rely fully upon Him. He exhorts Israel to submit to the secret counsel of God and trust Him to work all things together for the ultimate good of the human race, according to His eternal plan.

"Even youths grow tired," Isaiah says (40:30), referring to military youths who are usually the picture of strong, young manhood. Without God's enabling, youth in itself will have no answers to life's problems; youth will utterly fail. "But those who hope in the Lord will . . . soar on wings like eagles; they will run and not grow weary, they will walk and not be faint" (v. 31).

The picture the prophet uses—that of the eagle—is pure joy in itself. The eagle speaks of an ability to be airborne, to soar above. With swift efficiency, the bird rises to heights unknown to man. The ancient world believed that the eagle never died. It certainly lived a longer life than most birds. The idea is that those who trust and have confidence in the Lord will be vigorous like the eagle until their most advanced years.

So where does this leave you and me? Have you hung up your joy on some trouble tree? Would you like to learn how to sing one of the songs of Zion in a foreign land? Would you love to laugh again? Wait on God patiently to give you His strength that never gives out, and sing the Babylonians a song of testimony to His power in your life. They need to see the joy of the Lord and come to Him! After all, God died in Christ for the whole world—Babylonians included. Perhaps they haven't rejected the Lord; it could be they haven't had a very good reason to accept Him!

•TALKING IT OVER•

1. Read Psalm 137 and discuss: *10 minutes*
   ☐ How humanly impossible it is to rejoice in these circumstances.
   ☐ How possible it is with Christ!

2. Circle the trouble tree where you are most likely to   *10 minutes*
   lose your joy. Discuss.
   The Gripe, Grief, Growth, Guilt, or Grind tree.

3. Read Isaiah 40.   *10 minutes*
   ☐ What do you learn about God?
   ☐ Which aspect of His character helps you, and why?
   ☐ What do you learn about eagles?
   ☐ What do you learn about yourself?

•PRAYING IT THROUGH•

Suggested Times

---

1. Praise God for who He is
(i.e., different aspects of His character).

4 minutes

---

2. Pray about the aspect of His character which
   ☐ You need to experience.
   ☐ A friend needs to experience.

4 minutes

---

3. Pray for children you know who—like the little ones in Psalm 137—are innocent victims of their circumstances.

4 minutes

---

4. Pray for a *message song* to sing to the Babylonians in your life.

4 minutes

---

5. Pray for friends or family members who have lost their joy through:
   ☐ grief
   ☐ guilt
   ☐ griping

4 minutes

•DIGGING DEEPER•

Isaiah 40:27-31

1. What two complaints did Israel and Judah, the Northern and Southern Kingdoms, have against the Lord? (Isa. 40:27) From what you have learned about their current situation, why might they have made these inaccurate assessments? (cf. Gen. 12:23, 28; 13:15)

2. Isaiah responds to their complaint with what two rhetorical questions? What should they have known about their God?

3. An important principle for correctly understanding the Bible is to keep in mind that Scripture often interprets Scripture. See Isaiah 40:28 and following. How does Isaiah answer his own questions? List each noun and verb describing God's character and His activity.

4. Recalling that God is eternal and "the Creator of the ends of the earth" (v. 28) would have reminded God's accusers that He is in complete control of His creation and not limited by it. How do these factors discredit the complaints found in verse 27?

5. It is, therefore, impossible for God to grow tired or weary. What specific activities and purposes of God's nature would Isaiah be referring to here?

6. Some of the Lord's accusers believed that He had neglected them, had left them to take care of themselves, and had passed them by. But, in contrast to being weary of well-doing, Isaiah describes God as the One who gives strength to the weary. What else does he say in verse 29 that God will do for those who are suffering?

7. Verse 29 should have reminded the complainants of what events and examples in Israel's history of God strengthening the weak and rescuing His people?

8. Even choice young men in the prime of life and physical prowess tire and stumble, but this is not true of God nor of whom else? In verse 31 the word "but" alerts the reader to what contrast?

9. How are we to demonstrate our hope in the Lord? To help answer this question, you may want to do a word study of *hope,* especially as it was used in the Old Testament and by Isaiah.

10. What is the promise to those who patiently wait for God's promises and purposes to come to pass?

11. The word "renew" means to change or exchange. What is being exchanged for what in verse 31?

12. Eagles rise in the air and sail through the skies effortlessly, it appears. With no apparent effort, what could God's people rise above in Isaiah's time and today in the strength the Lord provides?

Reflection

1. Do you believe God's ways are always right, even though you may not be able to understand them?

2. What circumstances are overwhelming you? As you hope in the Lord, trust Him for the strength to rise above these difficulties.

For Further Study

1. Memorize Isaiah 40:31.
2. Read an evangelical commentary or two on Psalm 137.

•TOOL CHEST•
(A Suggested Optional Resource)

HOW LONG, O LORD?
Reflections on suffering and evil. D.A. Carson, author of *How Long, O Lord?* (Baker), is a contemporary evangelical New Testament scholar known for his brilliant mind, the integrity by which he studies and treats the Scriptures, as well as his pastoral heart and gentle application of God's Word to God's people. God's sovereignty threads its way from page to page of this tool, yet with tender appreciation for the doubts and questions which pain and suffering elicit from our frail human hearts. Each chapter leaves the reader with hope for the future and a handful of questions for probing and digesting the deep spiritual truths within. *How Long, O Lord?* helps us grope with what C.S. Lewis so accutely defined as *The Problem of Pain* (Macmillan). The reader will finish this book with a sense of well-being and a heart enabled to whisper, "It is well with my soul."

6

Learning to Light the Way

•FOOD FOR THOUGHT•

The forces of darkness appeared to be winning. Jerusalem had been destroyed and Israel's God had been humbled in the eyes of the nations. Jehovah announced to the nation that He had called His Servant to vindicate and restore His honor. "Here is My Servant," He said. Most evangelicals believe the role of the Servant of the Lord was fulfilled in Jesus Christ.

This Servant, we are told, had been *elected* by Jehovah—the word means "specially chosen." He was to be a trusted envoy, a confidential representative. Jehovah delighted in this One and promised to put His Spirit on Him. The giving of the Spirit would set Him apart for His "real" work. And what was this "real" work? It was to bring justice to the nations. Jesus Christ, of course, fulfilled these prophecies of Isaiah as is told in Luke 4:16-21; Matthew 12:18-21; Mark 20:28, and many other places. He also said to His disciples one day, "As the Father has sent Me, I am sending you" (John 20:21). And again, "As My Father sent Me into the world, I have sent you into the world." How is this meant to affect our lives?

Well, every morning along with the cornflakes and newspaper, there should be a sense in every disciple's heart that, whatever our occupations, today we are His trusted envoys! We represent a head of state, carrying out His wishes and commands! This will necessitate our being willing and obedient to fulfill our duties.

It's hard, however, to represent your King in the middle of a hostile environment. In recent days, we have seen ambassadors in unfriendly countries treated at best with scant respect, and at worst, with ridicule and expulsion.

God's trusted envoy, however, "will not shout or cry out, or raise his voice in the streets" (Isa. 42:2). He will not contend but rather bring the word of reconciliation by gentle means. There will be a voluntary humility about God's servant that will forbid boasting. Christ's ministry, as we see it in the Gospels, was in fact humble, quiet, and unhysterical. I ask myself: Is mine?

We attain this sweet servant spirit when our hearts are set on His approval, and our souls are set on delighting Him. Oh, that we might grow spiritually enough to want to delight Him rather than expecting Him to delight us! Why did the Father so approve and delight in His servant Son? Because He knew His Son so delighted in His Father's will and work. In the words of a contemporary chorus,

> Take joy, my King, in what You hear:
> May it be a sweet, sweet sound in Your ear.

Not only was God's servant elected and precious, but He was endowed with the Holy Spirit. Jesus spoke with His Father's authority. He said, "The words I say to you are not just My own. Rather, it is the Father, living in Me, who is doing His work" (John 14:10). And what did Jesus say to His disciples? "All authority in heaven and on earth has been given to Me" (Matt. 28:18). So because the Holy Spirit would endow Him with power, the servant would be encouraged when things were difficult. Yes, He would be sent and spent; yet He would not fail or be discouraged till He had brought forth justice with truth. God's Servant will have staying power. Jesus had His moments of discouragement, yet Jehovah promised, "He shall not flag or break till the work is finished!" Rest assured what God did for Jesus, Jesus will do for us.

Jesus plowed His way through it all, from Bethlehem to Golgotha. Jehovah promised of Him, "A bruised reed He will not break, and a smoldering wick He will not snuff out" (Isa. 42:3). The calamus plant is a reed with a hollow stem. It is easily snapped by a wild animal or even a bird. It was used as a symbol of brittleness, of fragile weakness. Jesus was bruised but never broken.

Perhaps you have been bruised by disappointments, by a hard marriage, or rebellious kids. Perhaps it is the church or workmates that have trampled you underfoot. Many folk have suffered such bruisings; their whole psyche is red, raw, tender, and inflamed, needing an ice pack. Yet God promises us that even if we are so terribly bruised, we will never be broken.

To change the picture a little, He also promised we will be lit but never allowed to be extinguished. Perhaps we are burning so low some folks are wondering if we are lit at all. Maybe no one has cared for us enough to trim our wick! Yet He has promised, "A smoldering wick He will not snuff out." By the side of this particular Bible verse in my Bible, I have written, "It's tough—I've had enough—but please don't snuff!"

Maybe we need to spend a little time with the hymnbook and pray:

Breathe on me, Breath of God,
Fill me with life anew,
That I may love what Thou dost love,
And do what Thou wouldst do.

Jehovah God offered His servant His immediate assistance. "I will help thee—I will hold thee by thy hand," He promised. He Himself will be present with us at all times. What more can we possibly need?

The reed was used to play music or to give service to the writer as a pen. The lamp was to provide light to all in the house. We need to allow our God to play a sweet tune through our given lives, to use us as writing instruments, to trim our wicks and gently put His nail-pierced hands around our flickering flame, and fan it into flaming faith.

And how do we then encourage others? With the comfort we have been given: "Praise be to the God and Father of our Lord Jesus Christ, the Father of compassion and the God of all comfort, who comforts us in all our troubles, so that we can comfort those in any trouble with the comfort we ourselves have received from God" (2 Cor. 1:3-4).

Do we turn on a mighty blast of spiritual wind when presented with smoldering lamps and blow them quite out? Or do we treat such flagging servants with the tender breath of love, reminding them they are precious, elect, and endowed? In the measure that we encourage them as we ourselves have been encouraged, we are profitable servants.

Touch my stem, Lord—
Low I bend with bruisings—
Gently now, for I'm Thy damaged reed.
Break me not, my Promiser of Power.
Raise not Your voice; yet rather meet my need.

Speak tenderly that therapy of caring

May cool the angry swellings softly down—
Relieve the heat of hurts so deep and crushing,
I in the sea of them am like to drown.

So mend and mold me into stern believing
That shaped and sharpened, healed and held,
A pen I'll be,
To write your words of healed relieving
Within the hearts and lives of broken men.

from *Wings* (Victor Books, 1984)

•TALKING IT OVER•

1. Read Isaiah 42 over and share which part of it
   □ rebukes you;
   □ comforts you;
   □ challenges you.

   8 minutes

2. Read Luke 4:16-22.
   Why do you think the people in the synagogue were so amazed?

   7 minutes

3. Do you think of yourself as an elect, endowed servant?
   □ If so, why?
   □ If not, why?

   8 minutes

4. What can we do for ourselves when we are bruised or flickering?
   □ What can we do for others?
   □ How does God heal bruises in our life?

   7 minutes

• PRAYING IT THROUGH •

1. (On your own) Think about these statements: *10 minutes*
   ☐ God will not fail to take the pain out of the
   pounding.
   ☐ Jesus is God's perfect Servant to help us. He
   was bruised, but never broken. He will do for
   you what His Father did for Him.
   Read the prayer at the end of the narrative and
   make it your own.

2. (Together) Pray for bruised believers and flickering   *5 minutes*
   followers in the church, the mission field,
   parachurch work.

3. (Together) Read Isaiah 42.   *5 minutes*
   Pray some of the verses for people you know.
   (E.g., v. 1 — "Lord, help _____ to realize he is cho-
   sen by You to be Your servant.")

•DIGGING DEEPER•

Isaiah 42:1-4

1. Who is introduced in Isaiah 42:1-4? What description is given of Him? What is His work, and how will He accomplish it?

2. Compare the other "Servant songs" in Isaiah (cf. 49:1-6; 50:4-9; and 52:13–53:12). What more do you learn about the Servant of the Lord?

3. See Isaiah 41:21ff. With whom is the Servant of the Lord contrasted? Israel's attention has been focused on whom or what?

4. What special relationship does the Servant enjoy, and what words are used to depict it? What does the word "uphold" convey?

5. For what purpose has the Servant been endowed and equipped with the Spirit? How successful will He be in His mission?

6. The Servant will not only proclaim justice, but He will also cause judgment to be brought about to the entire world (see 42:1, "to the nations"). Is His work characterized as condemnatory or evangelistic in verses 2-4? Support your answer from the text.

7. Contrast the Servant to false prophets and world conquerors known in Israel's history.

8. The Servant of the Lord is a messianic figure. How did the Lord Jesus fulfill Isaiah 42:1-4? Give New Testament references in support of your answer.

9. How do the two word pictures in Isaiah 42:3 characterize the nature of the Messiah's work and ultimately the nature of the One who sent Him?

10. Do you know anyone weak, fragile, broken, or oppressed? How could they benefit from the Servant's ministry?

11. What idea is repeated three times in verses 1-4, and why?

12. What might be delaying the Messiah's global mission? What can we be certain of, according to Isaiah 42:4?

13. The Servant's law is the Gospel. Hope is typically associated with the Gospel. Give examples from the Book of Acts of islands and coastlands putting their hope in the Servant's law.

14. How are Isaiah's two predominant themes threaded through 42:1-4?

Reflection

1. What puny notions and ideas consume your thoughts? Try diverting your attention to the Lord Jesus and His mission several times a day this week when you catch yourself thinking about worthless things.

2. What instrument has the Lord Jesus chosen to accomplish His work on earth? How are you establishing justice? What is your personal part to play in world evangelism?

3. Do you believe the whole world will eventually submit to Christ's universal rule? How may Isaiah 42:1-4 help you?

For Further Study

1. Memorize Isaiah 42:3.
2. Do a study of Isaiah's use of the word "servant." How many meanings does it have? Which meaning suits Isaiah 42:1 best?

•TOOL CHEST•
(A Suggested Optional Resource)

A GUIDE TO SELECTING AND USING BIBLE COMMENTARIES
A Guide to Selecting and Using Bible Commentaries (Word) by Douglas Stuart introduces the reader to the validity of acquainting oneself with Bible commentaries. Golden rules for commentary selection and usage are also contained within this resource. Categories are offered to help the Bible student choose the commentary that best fits his or her situation. Over half of the work is a selected commentary list, somewhat like a bibliography of over 1,100 commentaries on the books of the Bible. A chapter is also dedicated to major commentary series, with a brief description and critique of each.

7
Learning to Lead

• FOOD FOR THOUGHT •

An intense young man going into ministry asked a leader for some word of advice. Looking at his earnest, young face, the leader thought a touch of humor might help. "Well," he said "you'll undoubtedly need the heart of a child, the mind of a scholar, and the skin of a rhinoceros." Puzzled, the young man computed the answer and then hesitantly smiled. "It's all right to laugh," the leader encouraged him gently; "that's my advice!"

We surely need to be able to laugh at ourselves and not to take ourselves too seriously if we are to hang in there for the long haul; but there is obviously more to it than having a good laugh every day. The Scriptures give us a pretty good model of the perfect servant leader in Isaiah 50. For each of us in full-time Christian work and also for those in lay service in the church, this chapter describes God's perfect servant leader—the coming Messiah. This is the One that God would send in order to serve mankind by accomplishing people's redemption and leading them into life. Christians believe this holy person, here described, is Jesus of Nazareth. One day this Jesus said to His disciples, "The Son of man did not come to be served, but to serve" (Matt. 20:28); and again, "As the Father has sent Me, I am sending you" (John 20:21). So let's examine Isaiah's description of a perfect servant leader in this particular Scripture, and see what we can apply to our own lives and service for Him.

First, a perfect servant leader needs to have "the tongue of a teacher" (Isa. 50:4, NEB). Immediately some of us will be tempted to say (perhaps with some sense of relief), "Teaching isn't my gift." But it doesn't say the "gift" of a teacher; it says the "tongue" of one.

The *New International Version* says "an instructed tongue," and the *King James Version* says "that I may know how to speak a word in season to him that is weary." The Lord God has promised us the know-how to know what to say to help others. This is a promise not just for the up-front type of teacher but for every disciple. In fact, a disciple is exactly what the Lord God has in mind, as He goes on to say through the prophet that He will whisper the words we need to know and how to say them directly into our spiritual ear! In other words, He will help us to develop "the ear of a disciple." The *New English Bible* renders this verse, "He sharpened my hearing that I might listen like one who is taught" (50:4).

He longs to help us to develop the holy humility of habitually having an open ear heavenward. The true teachers are those who are ever conscious that they must be taught themselves before presuming to teach others. Not to develop this humility leads to Pharisaism, which Paul sharply rebuked by saying to these proud people, "You, then, who teach others, do you not teach yourself?" (Rom. 2:21)

If I am to "be prepared to give an answer to everyone who asks [me] to give the reason for the hope that [I] have" (1 Peter 3:15), then I will certainly need to be busy studying "to present [myself] to God as one approved" (2 Tim. 2:15). Then, like Jesus, I will "be about my Father's business" (Luke 2:49, KJV).

Am I teachable? Am I eager to be a servant leader who is effective in other people's lives? Whose lives? The lives of people who are described here as "the weary." The Bible says that God's servant will know how to give a word to the weary (see Isa. 50:4).

Once we are eager to be taught, the Lord God will soon present us with pupils! This world is so full of weary, worn-out, sad human beings. He will have no problem at all linking us up. He just wants us to be available—every day.

This availability will undoubtedly require expendability on our part. We will have to be up early in the day to receive our instructions from the Lord, realizing that in all probability the word we receive will be needed by another before the day is through. As the little chorus goes,

> In the morning first of all,
> Savior, let me hear Thy call.
> Make me ready to obey
> Thy commands throughout the day.

"He wakens me morning by morning, wakens my ear to listen like one being taught," says Isaiah (50:4b).

Our words will need to come out of our worship! Faced with people problems, my own best thoughts will be silly at best and stupid at worst because in the end only His word endures forever! A few years ago, catching the importance of this, I penned a poem:

> Give my words wings, Lord.
> May they alight gently on the branches of men's minds
> bending them to the winds of Your will.
> May they fly high enough to touch the lofty,
> low enough to breathe the breath
> of sweet encouragement upon the downcast soul.
>
> Give my words wings, Lord
> May they fly swift and far,
> Winning the race with the word of the worldly wise,
> to the hearts of men.
>
> Give my words wings, Lord.
> See them now
> nesting—
> down at Thy feet.
> Silenced into ecstasy,
> home at last.
>
> from *Wings* (Victor Books, 1984)

I learned that my words would never win the race with the words of the worldly wise to the hearts of men if I hadn't first truly worshiped. Even Jesus, God's perfect servant, said, "I do nothing on My own but speak just what the Father has taught Me" (John 8:28).

So the Lord God promises to give the tongue of a teacher and the ear of a disciple to His servants to "know how to speak a word in season to him that is weary" (KJV); or as The *New English Bible* renders the verse, "skill to console the weary with a word in the morning." May I reverently add, in the afternoon, evening, or even into the night! In season and out of season, I can bank on the Lord God giving me a suitable needed word.

Think what this will mean to the single parent, the adult child of an alcoholic, an infertile couple desperately longing for children, the Christian who has fallen into sin and sees no hope of restoration! The know-how to know what to say is ours, and even to know when to say it.

This is where obedience comes in. God's perfect servant leader says He will not disobey or turn back in defiance (Isa. 50:5). If we are eager and willing, He will help us to have an obedient heart like His. God's perfect servant set His face like a flint and pressed on to do the Father's will. He became obedient to death, even the death of the cross (Phil. 2:8).

Learning to lead means learning to follow, to commit ourselves to Him fully and to His plan for us to reach our world. Helping people takes time—all of your time, because people-helpers are in very short supply. The motivation for such selfless listening, loving, and leading is undoubtedly an understanding of Jesus our model, and an overwhelming sense of gratitude for what He did for us on the cross. This leads us to give ourselves unreservedly to Him.

One day I worshiped, studied, and meditated on verses from Psalm 139. "If I say, 'Surely the darkness will hide me and the light become night around me,' even the darkness will not be dark to You; the night will shine like the day, for darkness is as light to You" (vv. 11-12).

I thought about my own personal fears of the dark stemming from an overactive imagination. I had opened my ear to hear like one being taught over the years, and learned that a disciple of Jesus fears not the darkness when He who is the light of the world lives in his or her life. I thought about the time when we were first married, and my husband was in business and traveled a lot. It was hard to get into bed without looking under it! (I have to admit it can still be a struggle 33 years later!) I would read and read and read well past midnight before putting off the light and having to face the darkness. Sometimes I never would switch the light off till morning. As I recalled my very real fears in this regard, I began to make a list of all the promises of God concerning this particular fear that He had given me over time. Peace, comfort, and praise filled my heart as I recalled many of those precious promises and how He had helped me overcome my anxiety.

That very day after this particular personal worship time in Psalm 139, as I went about my business, it was as if God gathered all the people who were afraid of the dark in my entire neighborhood and brought them to me! I found myself talking to an old lady I knew who was living alone and was extremely nervous at night. Then I had lunch with an air hostess who, in the course of conversation, told me of an incident when she was eleven and alone at night when a thief entered the house. She rang the police and hid under the bed till they came. A brave little girl, I thought—but she added as a postscript, "Ever since then I've been so afraid of the dark!" There was a student I bumped into later that day who worked third shift, putting herself through school. She had to ride her bike home in the dark very late at night. And there was a mother whose husband traveled just like mine who dreaded the clock chiming 10 P.M.

The Lord God, having met with His disciple (me) in the morning and having given me a word in season for people weary with the fear of the dark, helped me be an obedient servant and bring His word of comfort and help to my friends, leading them into life! It was a wonderful day! I know He intends every one of our ordained days to be the same (Ps. 139:16).

•TALKING IT OVER•

1. (Group discussion) Before you read Isaiah 50, did you think of yourself as a disciple, teacher, and counselor? Do you now?

   10 minutes

   Share an example of someone who has consoled you when you were weary, or someone you have been able to console. What did they say, or what did you say?

2. (On your own) Have a worship time.

   12 minutes

   ☐ Be still and know that He is God.
   ☐ Read Psalm 139.
   ☐ Choose a verse that strikes you. Shut your eyes in order to concentrate and figure out why that particular verse arrested your attention.
   ☐ What do you think the verse you chose is saying?
   ☐ What do you think it is saying *to you?*
   ☐ Pray about it.
   ☐ Ask God to help you put it into practice in your life.
   ☐ Expect God to have you pass this thought on to someone else who needs it today or this week.

   Share your thoughts with the group.

3. Share any helpful tools or methods you have developed to enhance your own personal worship time.

   8 minutes

•PRAYING IT THROUGH•

*Suggested
Times*

1. (On your own) Meditate.
   Open your Bible to Isaiah 50:4-5. Read it, then
   think about Jesus. Think about Him teaching people about God, comforting the weary, counseling
   the hurting—being obedient.

   4 minutes

2. Articulate.
   Spend time praying short prayers for yourself, that
   you might be like Him.

   4 minutes

3. (With the group) Propagate.
   Think of weary, hurting people. Bring their needs
   to God in prayer (first names only). Ask Him how
   you might help them.

   4 minutes

4. Pray for the servant leaders in your church, that
   they may learn to do all the things in Isaiah 50:4-5.

   4 minutes

•DIGGING DEEPER•

Isaiah 50:4-9

1. After reading Isaiah 50:4-9, examine a Bible dictionary or commentary to determine the setting of this passage.

2. How do these verses connect with their surrounding context of chapters 49–53?

3. The word *servant* is omitted from Isaiah 50:4-9, but many Bible scholars suggest the passage applies to the Servant of the Lord since it is similar to the other Servant songs of Isaiah (42:1-4; 49:1-6; 52:13–53:12), and is written in first person. What do you think?

4. What caricature depicts the Servant in Isaiah 50:4?

5. What specific ministry or mission has the Servant been given? By whose authority is He to carry it out?

6. How is the Servant's mission like what we read in Isaiah 42:1-4?

7. Knowing what you do of the background of this passage, identify the weary ones and the accusers.

8. What body parts are employed as one-word illustrations in these verses, and to teach what lessons?

9. In the face of torment and violent opposition, how does the Servant conduct Himself? Wherein lies His confidence?

10. What was the purpose of the afflictions from the vantage point of the accusers? Did they achieve their intended results?

11. These atrocities were performed on the Prophet Isaiah. From the following New Testament parallels, what broader fulfillment did they have? (cf. Matt. 27:26, 30-31; John 19:1)

12. Who were the weary ones the Lord Jesus sustained? (cf. Matt. 5:3-10; 11:28) Who were His accusers? (give references with your answer)

13. What truth do the two illustrations in Isaiah 50:9b express? Is Isaiah speaking of immediate destruction or ultimate, definitive, and eternal judgment? Which is more important? Did the prophet see the prediction fulfilled in his lifetime?

Reflection

1. Is it your desire to be instructed by the Lord and illumined by His Spirit so that you too might have a learned tongue? What was the pupil's responsibility in Isaiah 50:4, and what is yours?

2. What gifts has God given you? Are they serving His purposes or your selfish ambitions? (Phil. 2:3)

3. How did the Prophet Isaiah and the Servant of the Lord prepare for ministry? Is it possible to be a blessing to the hurting and oppressed without first being obedient to the Lord? Would your close friends describe you as having an obedient disposition?

4. Like a diamond, a flint is a hard rock. Are you easily sidetracked from God's direction and purposes? Pray to be more like Christ.

5. Neither Isaiah nor the Servant reacted to pressure by defending themselves, but allowed the Lord God to vindicate and pronounce them just. Are you given to defending yourself?

For Further Study

1. Memorize Isaiah 50:4-5.
2. Read all of Isaiah 50 and contrast Israel and the Servant. Whom are you more like?

•TOOL CHEST•
(A Suggested Optional Resource)

NIV WOMEN'S DEVOTIONAL BIBLE
Zondervan has now designed an *NIV Women's Devotional Bible* to encourage women in their daily reading and study of Scripture. A Bible passage is designated for each day of the week, followed by an inspirational devotional written on that day's Bible passage or on a topic related to the passage. Additional Scripture readings are also referenced and a key verse is highlighted for each day of the week. The devotionals have been authored by more than 100 prominent Christian women, most of whom lived within the last century. A one-year Bible reading plan is provided along with a subject index. You could choose to study one of Isaiah's themes and find devotionals and their corresponding page numbers listed under your subject. A special feature is the "Weekending" section, which has a brief poem or prose and two short Bible readings for Saturday and Sunday. This resource may help spruce up your own devotional life or a friend's.

8
Learning to Lay Down Our Lives

•FOOD FOR THOUGHT•

Jesus talked about taking up our cross and following Him (Matt. 16:24). The Apostle Paul, writing to the Philippians, told them, "For it has been granted to you on behalf of Christ not only to believe on Him, but also to suffer for Him" (Phil. 1:29). The Lord reminded His disciples, "Greater love has no one than this, that he lay down his life for his friends." Then He added, "You are My friends if you do what I command" (John 15:13-14). He laid down His life for us; we must die daily for Him. How do we do that? By daily dying to our own interests so we can serve others.

Laying down our life doesn't sound awfully exciting to Westerners, who regard life as a right. And yet, the Bible teaches that we die to live, we give to get. "Unless a kernel of wheat falls to the ground and dies, it remains only a single seed," said Jesus. "But if it dies, it produces many seeds" (John 12:24). Actually, there is really no way to enter into His legacy of life, love, laughter, and light without putting this particular principle into operation.

In Isaiah 53, the perfect servant lays down His perfect life so that we imperfect people may live life to the full here and now, and in eternity after this life is over. Let's look at this chapter to see how He did this, in order to follow His example of humility and sacrifice. Isaiah begins this famous passage by asking the people if they believe his report: his great good news about salvation. He explains that God's suffering servant will come to earth to accomplish this salvation for us, and would have humble beginnings like a root or stump out of parched ground. However, He would grow up before His Father like a tender plant until He reached the stature of a cedar of Lebanon! Jesus understood Isaiah 53 referred to Him, that it was His Scripture. He believed as God's righteous servant that He was going to justify many because He would bear their sins. In Luke 22:37 He said, "I tell you that this must be fulfilled in Me." John Stott comments, "It was from this chapter more than from any other that he learnt that the vocation of the Messiah was to suffer and die for human sin and so be glorified" (*The Cross of Christ*, InterVarsity). "I must suffer many things," He said; and again, "[I haven't] come to be served, but to serve, and give [my] life as a ransom for many" (Matt. 20:28). Verses 13-15 of Isaiah 53 speak of the indignities this wonderful servant would suffer. People would be startled by His appearance. His sufferings would so disfigure Him He would hardly look human. He would be "like one from whom men hide their faces" (53:3). No one likes to see people suffer or to even be around people that do. Jesus knew isolation because of His calling.

It's hard to think of following Christ down this path. No one likes to suffer or would choose to. Yet as a Romanian pastor put it, "It's inevitable for the Christian." The cross caused Jesus loneliness and solitariness—a bitter affliction to the Eastern man. In his culture, to experience *shalom*—peace and security—a man must have the support of his family and neighbors. Yet God's Messiah would be despised and rejected by His society, said Isaiah. So may we be if we follow the Master.

In fact, to be a follower of Christ we must avoid all the things our society worships. Jesus had no beauty or majesty to attract us to Him (53:2), no regal pomp, no splendid surroundings. In fact, His appearance was not flashy, His clothes being Galilean homespun—nothing out of the ordinary at all. Yet He had a spiritual beauty, a quiet calm, and holy majesty that could be discerned by the spiritual. In the world's eyes He was a loser; and so might we be for His sake. If we are enslaved to the literal, temporal, and earthy, then we are not following Christ!

Not only would the Messiah fail the people in their expectations of another sort of person—a Jewish king or a patriot like Judas Maccabeus—but He would insist on living a simple life on the wrong side of the tracks. He would be untrained, unlearned, and what is more, He would have doubtful parentage. "We know who *our* Father is," the Pharisees jibed. "You do dishonor Me," Jesus replied, rebuking them.

Someone has said that if Jesus lived in our society today, He would be told He needed therapy! So many of the self-oriented notions purported to be "the way" to go in our day and age were denounced by Jesus.

"Surely," said Isaiah, contemplating His sufferings, "He took up our infirmities and carried our sorrows, yet we considered Him stricken by God" (53:4). Those who saw Christ suffer imagined He was suffering at the hands of God for His own sins. All who ever endured unjust punishment can look at the cross, see a suffering God, lay their heads on His breast, and know He understands.

Isaiah tells us He was "crushed" for our iniquities. There is no word used in Scripture that tells more of the severity of the Savior's sufferings than this one. First He was "crushed" by the rejection of His family and friends, and then by the mighty crushing rejection of God Himself. The chastisement which brought us peace—which put an end to the enmity between man and an offended God—was upon Him; and with His wounds we are healed (53:5).

We must never forget this. Paul didn't, and saints down through the ages haven't either. Paul said, "I bear on my body the marks of Jesus" (Gal. 6:17). Amy Carmichael wrote:

Has thou no scar?
No hidden scar on foot, or side, or hand?
I hear thee sung as mighty in the land,
I hear them hail thy bright ascendant star,
Hast thou no scar?

Hast thou no wound?
Yet I was wounded by the archers, spent,
Leaned Me against a tree to die; and rent
By ravening beasts that compassed Me, I swooned:
Hast *thou* no wound?

No wound? no scar?
Yet, as the Master shall the servant be,
And pierced are the feet that follow Me;
But thine are the whole: can he have followed far
Who has nor wound nor scar?

from "Toward Jerusalem"

What an encouragement to those crushed in spirit to know He knows! David, understanding this, said in Psalm 34:18, "The Lord is close to the brokenhearted and saves those who are crushed in spirit." Now all that remains is for us to believe Isaiah's report for ourselves and make sure the rest of the world believes it too!

All of us need to recall that the essence of sin is to go our own way rather than God's way, and that the Lamb of God, Jesus Christ, was slaughtered because of our waywardness in order to bring us back to God (Isa. 53:6, 12). All of us are black sheep. There was ever only one white sheep in the whole history of mankind—Jesus Himself. He didn't turn to His own way but rather went God's way. Twenty-eight times in the Book of Revelation Jesus is identified with *this lamb* who had our sin laid on Him and was sacrificed for us.

Isaiah 53 tells us about His unjust treatment (v. 8) and the fact that He would die childless. To die without children was considered a tragedy in His culture, yet this was part of the price He paid for our redemption. He was "cut off"—taken away before His time, and made His grave with the wicked (v. 9).

The miracle of prophecy (history written in advance) tells us that Jesus Christ—in His birth, life, and death—fulfilled all these things written about Himself hundreds of years before they even happened. How can we not believe He was God's servant, born to die for us?

Do we acknowledge that God made Him a scapegoat—a guilt offering for us? John Stott wrote, "This does not mean God compelled Jesus to do what He was unwilling to do Himself. Jesus was not the unwitting victim of God's harsh justice. Jesus did pay the price for sin but God was active in Christ doing it and Christ freely played His part" (e.g., Heb. 10:5-10) [*The Cross of Christ*, InterVarsity). Bishop Stephen Neill says, "If the crucifixion of Jesus . . . is in some way, as Christians have believed, the dying of God Himself, then . . . we can understand what God is like" (*The Cross of Christ*, InterVarsity).

Isaiah 53 does not leave God's suffering servant hanging on the cross. "He will see His offspring and prolong His days, and the will of the Lord will prosper in His hand," exults the prophet (v. 10). He will be head of a spiritual prosperity (you and me). "After the suffering of His soul, He will see the light of life and be satisfied" (v. 11). He will be abundantly compensated by the joy of a progressive work of salvation in the hearts of men.

In other words, God's servant can think of the cross—think about those of us who will accept His death on our behalf—and say, "It was worth it—it was all worth it." And what sort of lives should we live in order to hear Him whisper these incredible words to our souls? A life like His. We cannot die for men's sins or even our own; but we can die to our selfish lifestyle, attitudes, and actions and serve the people around us! We cannot ever know the sufferings He suffered, but we can bring pleasure to His heart by bearing reproach and rebuke willingly and cheerfully as He did, if need be. If we indeed take up our cross and follow Him, we can know that as God rewarded His servant

Jesus, He will one day reward us by including us in the inheritance the Father has ordained for His Son. And wonder of wonders—on the way home, God's marvelous Servant promises He will pray for us! (v. 16) When we were so lost in sin and there was no one to pray for us—He did! He promises to continue that ministry of intercession.

So in closing, it is not a man's sins that keep him from God, but his unwillingness to have them forgiven! Many in our world don't even know that this is possible. If we are to believe Isaiah's report, we will first ask God to forgive us, and then spend the rest of our lives making sure others have the chance to choose to be forgiven also! So let us get on with our lives with the love of Isaiah's suffering servant in our hearts and with the invitation of the Lord upon our lips:

" 'Come now, let us reason together,' says the Lord. 'Though your sins are like scarlet, they shall be as white as snow; though they are red as crimson, they shall be like wool' " (Isa. 1:18).

• TALKING IT OVER •

*Suggested
Times*

1. Read the whole of Isaiah 53 over carefully and prayerfully.

8 minutes

2. Look up Leviticus 5:15-16; 6:5.
   What do these verses tell you about a scapegoat?

7 minutes

3. Read Hebrews 10:5-10.
   Discuss: God and Christ took the initiative together to save sinners.

8 minutes

4. Read Philippians 2:6-8.
   Which part of this passage touches you, and why?

7 minutes

•PRAYING IT THROUGH•

Suggested Times

1. (On your own)   *5 minutes*
   ☐ Meditate on one part of Isaiah 53.
   ☐ Respond in prayer to what you read.

2. (Corporately)   *15 minutes*
   ☐ Pray that you will understand the Cross more
      thoroughly. Pray that . . .
         your family will understand
         your neighbors will understand
         your world will understand
   ☐ Pray that you will follow Christ by laying down
      your life for . . .
         your family
         your friends
         your enemies
   ☐ Think back over the lessons in this study.
   ☐ Praise God for the Book of Isaiah and for all the
      things you have learned from it!

• DIGGING DEEPER •

Isaiah 53:1-12

1. Why is astonishment expressed in Isaiah 53:1?

2. "The arm of the Lord" is synonymous with the Lord's strength. What, according to verse 1, have men been strengthened and empowered by the Lord to do? Is it possible to do so apart from the Lord's enablement?

3. The Servant grew up or appeared before the Lord; that is, His life was lived in the presence of the Lord God. What does this teach us about our God?

4. Dry ground is not a favorable condition for growth and nourishment of plants. What does this picture imply about the servant's background or upbringing? What does it suggest about His future?

5. What unique features and qualities did the Servant possess which attracted others to Him and helped further His mission?

6. Beyond the physical appearance of the Servant, what is intended in 53:2-3? (cf. Phil. 2:5-11)

7. The sorrows and sufferings found in 53:3 included physical pain and sickness. Many people probably believed the Servant suffered for the sins He committed (v. 4). Recall the life of Christ. How was it that so many Jews and Gentiles misjudged the Servant and did not recognize Him? Try to substantiate your answer from the Gospels.

8. The original word for "carried" in verse 4 means "to lift up, to bear, to take away." What are some of the consequences of sin? What does Isaiah predict the Servant can and will do with these consequences? (cf. 1 Peter 2:24)

9. Verse 5 begins with the word "but" to indicate a contrast. Verses 5-6 reveal the true reason for the Servant's suffering. What is it? They also explain who deserved the punishment He took upon Himself. Identify the guilty parties.

10. In fulfillment of these words (vv. 5-12), the Lord Jesus suffered a violent death and Himself bore the guilt and punishment of sin. For whose sins did God's judgment fall on Him? (v. 8) What were the results and benefits for those for whom He was stricken?

11. Why did the Servant have to suffer? Who was responsible for His suffering? Who is behind the scenes and ultimately in control of all that happens in this Servant song?

12. The Servant voluntarily endured His suffering. In what manner did He do so? (cf. 1 Peter 2:23) List all the things He suffered.

13. This song takes a triumphant turn in verse 10b. What is different? What promises are given to the Servant? What final promise is given in verse 12 to those for whom He suffered?

14. How are the themes of judgment and salvation brought to a climax in this final Servant song?

Reflection

1. Do you sometimes wonder if God is aware of your trials? Return to question 11. How can these truths help you trust God more in your misfortunes?

2. The Servant arose from a worst-case scenario, and no one foresaw the potential victory He would accomplish. Do you see any parallels in your own life?

3. How is peace with God to be obtained?

4. Are you a member of "My people" (v. 8) for whom the Servant was stricken? If you are uncertain, talk with your group leader and ask how you might be included among God's people and be justified before Him.

For Further Study

1. Review all eight chapters and write a paper on Isaiah, including all you have learned about the book and its message.
2. Study the Book of Isaiah in a Bible dictionary. What additional information can you add to your knowledge of the book?
3. Memorize Isaiah 53:5-6.

•TOOL CHEST•
(A Suggested Optional Resource)

CHRISTIAN FICTION

"Is there any fine fiction out there?" Maybe you have asked that same question. There is just no disappointment like sitting down for a few quiet moments with a promising novel, only to find several pages later that it is not very wholesome. You will find that the values in *The Zion Chronicles* (Bethany) by Bodie Thoene will not let you down. Set in the 1940s, the series dramatically recounts the birth of the state of Israel, and the spiritual pilgrimage of four young people whose lives are woven together by divine design. These historical novels will make you laugh, cry, and hold your breath as you begin to take a stab at understanding the Israeli-Arab conflict. Central to the story line is the discovery of the Isaiah scroll of the Dead Sea Scrolls. Cuddle up in a warm quilt for an evening and enjoy Book I: *The Gates of Zion* (Bethany).